The Hidden Treasure

Especially for Joan, Stanley and Mark
Stephanie Jeffs

For Alison, Emma and Katie
Steve Hicks

Edited by David Martin

BIBLE SOCIETY
Stonehill Green, Westlea, SWINDON SN5 7DG, England

Published in association with AD Publishing Services Ltd
7 Hill Side, Cheddington, Leighton Buzzard, LU7 SP

Copyright © 1991 AD Publishing Services Ltd
Text copyright © 1991 Stephanie Jeffs
Illustrations copyright © 1991 Steve Hicks

All rights reserved. No part of this publication may be reproduced, stored in a retrieval system, or transmitted, in any form or by any means, electronic, mechanical, photocopying, recording or otherwise without the prior permission of The British and Foreign Bible Society.

Unless otherwise stated, quotations from the Bible are from the Good News Bible, published by the Bible Societies/Collins, © American Bible Society, New York, 1966, 1971, 1976.

First published 1991

ISBN 0 564 08175 2

Printed in Hong Kong

The Hidden Treasure

Story by Stephanie Jeffs
Illustrated by Steve Hicks

'Yep!' said Hickory, as he looked out of the window. 'I'm sure there be gold in that there field!'

'So you said, Hickory Hicks, yesterday and the day before and the day before that. I be sick and tired of hearin' you talk of gold in that there field!' said Ma, as she sat in the rocking chair by the fire. 'There's plenty of other things you should be settin' your mind on...'

'But Ma,' said Hickory, 'I knows there's gold in that field!'

'How d'you know, Hickory? You just tell me how. Feel it in your bones, I suppose? Well feelin's in bones ain't gonna do us any good! Stop your day dreamin' and come down to earth while you can!'

Hickory smiled and patted the pocket of his patched trousers.

'I know it, Ma, an' I can prove it. This ain't no day dreamin', this be real!'

He reached into his pocket and took out a small round stone-like object. 'Look Ma, I found it. I found it in that field. It's gold, sure enough, real gold!'

Ma reached in the pocket of her apron and took out her spectacles. She held the nugget in her hands and looked at it closely. At last she spoke. 'Well, Hickory, that sure does look like gold!'

'Looks like gold, tastes like gold, and *is* gold! I tell you, Ma, we're gonna be rich!' Hickory clapped his hands with excitement and gave the rocking chair such a shove that Ma's spectacles slid off her nose into her lap.

'Stop your foolin' this instant! How's your findin' gold in that field gonna help us get rich? It might help ol' Solomon Scratch get richer, or have you forgot that field ain't our field, it's *his* field?'

'I knows that, Ma, but he don't know there's gold in his field. Anyway, I'm gonna buy us that field!'

'What with?' laughed Ma. 'Thin air?'

Later that night when Ma had gone to sleep, Hickory lay in bed thinking. At last he lifted up the corner of the lumpy old mattress and took out a small bag. He tipped the contents of the bag onto the bed, counted the collection of coins and sighed.

Taking the small candle across the room, Hickory opened the lid of a small, battered chest and dug his hands into it. He felt his way around the contents of the chest until he found

what he wanted. He pulled out an old sock, the toe of which contained something heavy.

Making his way towards the bed in the flickering candle light, Hickory tipped the coins from the sock and began to count again. When he had finished, he put all the coins under his mattress and, with another sigh, licked his fingers, snuffed out the candle, pulled the blanket over his head and settled down to sleep.

Hickory tossed and turned and tossed and turned, ploughing imaginary furrows in a golden field. With his plough he wrote, 'This field belongs to Hickory Hicks!'

    Hickory could not think of anything else but owning that field. At last he sat up.
    'Hickory,' he said to himself, 'this is the chance of a life-time! You *have* to buy that field! It don't matter how much it costs.'

When Ma woke up next morning, Hickory was already washed, dressed and shaven.

"Pon my soul!' said Ma. 'What you be dressed up for?'

'Ma,' said Hickory, 'I'm gonna see Solomon Scratch and ask if I can buy that field!'

Ma looked stern. 'It's mornin', Hickory Hicks, and high time you stopped this dreamin' nonsense. Wake up, and get on with somethin' that'll do us both some good!'

Hickory stared Ma straight in the eye. 'If I buys that field, Ma Hicks, it will do us some good. It'll be the best thing I ever do! I knows it for certain, an' nobody's goin' to make me change my mind.'

Ma sighed and slumped down into her rocking chair. 'You've gone soft in the head!' she said at last.

But Hickory didn't hear. He had already gone.

He felt confident as he rode into town.

'Mornin', Hick!' called Jed. 'You looks fine an' dandy!'

'I feels fine and dandy too!' replied Hickory.

'You gettin' wed?' laughed Old Turner as Hickory tethered his mare in the town square. 'I can't remember a time when I saw you lookin' so smart.'

'Nope,' replied Hickory, 'but I am gonna do somethin' special!'

'Now what'll that be, young Hickory?' replied Turner.

'You'll see,' smiled Hickory. 'You'll see soon enough.'

'Off to make your fortune, I suppose,' laughed the old man.

'Well maybe you're right,' said Hickory, as he left the old man chuckling to himself.

Now Hickory had never actually spoken to Solomon Scratch before. He had seen him riding through town and had heard many stories about him. Normally Hickory would not have dared to speak to him, but this morning he felt very confident.

'So, Mr Hicks,' said Solomon Scratch from behind his big oak desk, 'you want to buy my field?'

'Yes, sir,' said Hickory firmly. 'I surely do!'

Solomon Scratch took a large cigar from a silver box on his desk. He sniffed it thoughtfully, bit off the end and spat it onto the floor.

'I don't often get folks askin' to buy one of my fields, you know. An' it'll cost you, Mr Hicks. I ain't givin' away one of my fields for nothin'.'

'I know that, sir. I'll pay whatever it costs.'

'Will you, young man!' chuckled Scratch. 'An' just where's you gonna find the money?'

'I'll find it, sir,' said Hickory firmly. 'You name your price and I'll find the money.'

'Well, Mr Hicks, you sure are determined, I'll say that for you,' said Solomon Scratch as he pulled a large sheet of paper towards him. He dipped his pen in some ink and started to cover the page with figures. Eventually he stopped.

'Hmm,' said Scratch, puffing on a large cigar. 'You find me $200 and we got ourselves a deal!'

'Gee, thanks, Mr Scratch!' said Hickory, shaking him by the hand. '$200 it is!'

Hickory rode home as quickly as the old mare could manage.

'Ma!' he shouted. 'Mr Scratch'll sell us the field for $200! I told you we'll be rich!'

'$200!' shrieked Ma. 'Where'll we get that from?'

'We're gonna have ourselves an auction!' cried Hickory. 'We're gonna sell the house, sell the furniture, sell the horse and even sell your ol' rockin' chair! Then we'll have ourselves $200 and *then* we can buy ourselves the field!'

There was no stopping Hickory now. The thought of owning that field fired Hickory with an excitement he had never known before.

Word quickly spread through the town that Hickory was selling up – along with the rumours that Hickory had finally flipped his lid! But Hickory didn't care! Nothing else mattered apart from owning that field.

The sun shone brightly on the day of the auction. Hickory and Ma watched the long line of people, dressed in their best clothes, making their way towards the house.

'Fancy having all them folks a fingerin' me things!' grumbled Ma. 'I've never been so 'shamed in my life.'

'Don't you go frettin' yourself, Ma,' said Hickory. 'I knows it's difficult, but it'll be worth it.'

The auction itself went quickly, and Hickory watched as if in a dream as he saw the pile of dollars grow on the auctioneer's table.

'An' that,' said Mr Slickitt, the auctioneer, banging his gavel on the table for the last time, 'is the end of the auction.'

He thrust a pile of money into Hickory's hands. 'I thinks you'll find everythin' in order, sir. There's nothin' much left but here's your money, $196 and 14 cents – an' I've taken my fee!'

Hickory's hands clenched the notes tightly. His legs felt weak. 'But that ain't enough, Mr Slickitt, sir. I'm four dollars short!'

'Four dollars short in the head more like,' snapped Ma, rocking furiously in her chair which was by the front door.

'Quiet, Ma!' returned Hickory, and then added, 'Please! I gotta think.'

''Tis a bit late for thinkin' now,' mumbled Ma.

Hickory watched Ma and bit his lip, deep in thought. Suddenly he slapped his leg and ran over towards Ma.

'I've got it, Ma! Your chair! That was supposed to be in the sale.'

'An' what was I supposed to sit on, Hickory Hicks?' shouted Ma. But Hickory didn't hear. He pushed Ma out of the chair and left her standing in amazement.

'Mr Slickitt, Mr Slickitt,' cried Hickory. 'Wait a minute, Mr Slickitt. How d'you fancy a fine ol' rockin' chair in that office of yours?'

As the sun went down, Hickory and Ma sat in the middle of the field. The new people had already moved into the house and Ma could see the old mare trotting along the road behind her new owners. Everything had been sold – the beds, the blankets, even Hickory's sock!

'Well,' said Ma, 'you've been an' gone an' done it now, Hickory Hicks!'

'Yep!' said Hickory slowly. 'It sure was a close thing, Ma. 'Specially that last $4. An' Ma, I got something to tell you. This ain't no ordinary field. You take a look to see what's in it. Gold, Ma – more pieces than ever I thought. I've never been so happy in my whole life!'

Ma looked at Hickory real hard. 'An' everyone thought you was a fool. And you gott'n us all this. We didn't know the half of it.'

Credits

Story by Stephanie Jeffs
Pictures by Steve Hicks
Based on something much older...

The Story Behind the Story

'Let me tell you a story.' Teachers, parents and older friends often say this when asked to explain something. If it's a good story it will use things we know about to help us understand something more difficult or more important. Sometimes the story will include a riddle or puzzle to help us think more carefully. Many famous teachers have used this idea. Often the stories are called parables. The word means 'putting things side by side'.

The story you have read is based on a parable Jesus told nearly 2000 years ago. Many of the parables told by Jesus have become very famous. He used these stories to help people think differently about things.

He told this story to help those who could not understand why some people seemed to give up everything for something they believed in. He said that those who gave up things for God would be rewarded many times over.

'The Kingdom of heaven is like this. A man happens to find a treasure hidden in a field. He covers it up again, and is so happy that he goes and sells everything he has, and then goes back and buys that field.'

Matthew 13:44

Things to Notice About the Two Stories

When the man sold everything he owned just to buy a field, everyone thought he was a real fool.

At the time, the one who bought the field knew a lot more than everyone else – but he couldn't prove it for some time.

The one who bought the field had to give up a great deal and put up with a lot of hardship.

The joy of owning the treasure must have seemed greater when compared to all the hardship the man had to put up with in order to get it.

Thinking About It

'Hickory,' he said to himself, 'this is the chance of a life-time! You *have* to buy that field! It don't matter how much it costs.'

❑ *Hickory wanted to own the field more than anything else. Have you ever wanted anything that much? If so, what sort of thing?*

'We're gonna have ourselves an auction!' cried Hickory.

❑ *Hickory was prepared to sell everything in order to own the field – it was hard! What would you be willing to do so that you could have something you really wanted?*

❑ *Is there anything which would be just too difficult? How long would you be willing to wait?*

Word quickly spread through the town that Hickory was selling up – along with the rumours that Hickory had finally flipped his lid! But Hickory didn't care!

- *What does it feel like when everyone thinks you are foolish?*

- *What does it feel like when everyone thinks you are doing something foolish and you know you're not – but you can't prove it?*

> 'Gold, Ma – more pieces than ever I thought. I've never been so happy in my whole life!'

- *Hickory wanted to own the field because he knew that there was something very precious hidden in it. Some things are very precious and yet they cannot be bought or sold. What sort of things are these?*

- *What type of treasure would make you do what Hickory did?*